'No Cook' Children's Recipe Book

Recipes that Children Can Make on Their Own (or with just a little help from a grown-up)

Penelope R Oates

DISCLAIMER

All information in the book is for general information purposes only.

The author has used her best efforts in preparing this information and makes no representations or warranties with respect to the accuracy, applicability or completeness of the material contained within.

Furthermore, the author takes no responsibility for any errors, omissions or inaccuracies in this document. The author disclaims any implied or expressed warranties or fitness for any particular purpose.

The author shall in no event be held liable for losses or damages whatsoever. The author assumes no responsibility or liability for any consequences resulting directly or indirectly from any action or lack of action that you take based on the information in this document. Use of the publication and recipes therein is at your own risk.

Reproduction or translation of any part of this publication by any means, electronic or mechanical, without the permission of the author, is both forbidden and illegal. You are not permitted to share, sell, and trade or give away this document, it is for your own personal use only, unless stated otherwise.

The reader assumes full risk and responsibility for all actions taken as a result of the information contained within this book and the author will not be held responsible for any loss or damage, whether consequential, incidental, or otherwise that may result from the information presented in this book.

The author has relied on her own experiences when compiling this book and each recipe is tried and tested in her own kitchen.

By using any of the recipes in this publication, you agree that you have read the disclaimer and agree with all the terms.

IMPORTANT REMINDER: IT IS YOUR RESPONSIBILITY TO MAKE SURE YOUR CHILDREN ARE SAFE IN THE KITCHEN!!

Table of Contents

Introduction

Most children love to help with cooking and baking, I know mine did and now my grandchildren always want to make something when they visit.

In my day most children learned to cook by watching their parents and grandparents cooking with fresh ingredients bought the same day. But today, with the fast pace of life and so many fast food and convenience alternatives, a lot of children don't get the opportunity to learn how to cook.

This book is for people who want to find interesting and simple ways to allow their children to learn to cook and to encourage enthusiasm for food and cooking in later life.

I think we should encourage our children to take part in preparing meals as they are growing up. Maybe starting with something simple and fun like helping to mix a cake mixture and putting it into a cake pan ready for the oven, with the grownup dealing with ingredients and the oven. The children will take great pleasure in being able to say, "I made that..." and of course, in their mind, they did.

If we cook with our children we are in the enviable position of being able to help to shape their attitude to food and a healthy diet without it being obvious. Young children are like sponges and absorb information much more easily than a teenager or young adult, so if you teach them to cook healthy food from scratch as soon as you think they are interested, they may just take those lessons into their adult lives.

I recently read an interesting report that said;

"Indeed, cooking with kids can be the gift that keeps on giving; it has both short-term and long-term payoffs.

Some of the short-term benefits:

It encourages kids to try healthy foods. Kids feel like they are accomplishing something and contributing to the family. Kids are more likely to sit down to a family meal when they helped prepare it. Parents get to spend quality time with their kids. Kids aren't spending time in front of the TV or computer while they're cooking.

Kids generally aren't eating junk food when they're cooking a meal at home.

Some long-term benefits:

Learning to cook is a skill your children can use for the rest of their lives.
Kids who learn to eat well may be more likely to eat healthfully as adults.
Positive cooking experiences can help build self-confidence.
Kids who cook with their parents may even be less likely to abuse drugs..."

To see the full article - www.goo.gl/IVBmfy

I had to think a little about that last statement but I think it could refer to the fact that children who spend time actually *doing* things with the family, participating in family life, are less likely to take up with the wrong crowd who are making bad choices – but you may interpret that a different way...

Of course all learning should be fun and learning about food and cooking is no exception. So, although there are some healthy options to choose from in this book and a few recipes that need the help of an adult (for dealing with some equipment and hot stuff), I have also included some fun recipes children can make absolutely independent of adults.

Most of the recipes allow for you and your children to swap the ingredients around to include your own favorites, remember when you look at any recipe it is always open to change to suit your own tastes. For example, if you don't like coconut, try finely grated carrot with a little brown sugar added. Or, if you are not keen on dried cranberries, use chopped nuts. Encourage your children to use their imagination and creativity to come up with tasty alternative ingredients. In fact, that's how family favorites are born. So be bold and encourage your children to be adventurous.

You can show your children how to make finger food for family get-togethers or prepare nibbles for a sleep-over or a play date with minimum help from adults – and with that comes bragging rights! You provide the ingredients, the tools and suggestions – then stand back and watch the fun...

You could encourage your children to make a selection of the candies from this book and put them into a cellophane bag tied with pretty ribbon or a colorful box for handmade gifts for family and friends. Children just love to give gifts and are so proud if they've made them themselves.

There are a lot of sweet recipes in this book and I urge you to encourage your children to think of these as 'treats' rather than everyday food. You don't want your children to regard these fabulous candies and desserts as everyday food.

As your children get older and more safety conscious you can gradually allow more responsibility in the kitchen and let them deal with food mixers, knives (starting with a table knife for perhaps cutting sandwiches or a slice of cake) and using the microwave. It is up to you to decide when your children are responsible enough to move forward.

I have tried, where possible, to use American weights and measures (please forgive me if I get some wrong – I'm British...) but I have included a simple conversion chart at the end of the book for European readers.

Encouraging your children (remember that boys love to cook too...) to cook and enjoy the experience will be a memory for them to store in their subconscious life album and, you never know, you could find yourself with a budding Rachel Ray or Jamie Oliver!

Can I stress again that it is _your responsibility_ to make sure your children are SAFE in the kitchen!

Useful Stuff to Have When Cooking with Children

When you are cooking with children it is useful to have lots of different pieces of equipment to make the experience interesting and fun.

It doesn't have to cost a lot and you can improvise with a lot of things. For example, if you don't have a cookie cutter that will be the right size for cutting pastry for small tarts, you could find a cup that is the right size and use that. If you want a larger circle, use a plate to cut around. If you need to cut sandwiches, use a pizza cutter. Use your imagination and ask your children for suggestions too – you may be surprised at their inventiveness.

Below are a few suggestions for things you may want to get together for when you are cooking with children.

1. The most useful equipment I have in my collection of equipment for children is a selection of cookie cutters. They are not very expensive; in fact I recently bought a set of eight small cutters that I found in an online shop for £1.99 (around $3). For a cheap and cheerful set of all sorts of shapes and cutters, try looking at the PlayDoh range. Check Amazon to see a selection.

2. A selection of knives suitable for children to use. You can buy all sorts of sets specially made for children. Curious Chef have a lovely selection at Amazon.

3. An apron to keep clothes free of flour and sticky stuff! There are lots on offer that include an oven mitt and chef's hat.

4. Lots of different sprinkles, edible decoration, food colorings and flavorings.

5. If you are making candy for your children to give as a gift, it is good to have a selection of paper and foil candy cases at the ready.

6. Depending on the age of the children, a stable stool for them to stand on to reach the work surface safely.

Of course there are lots of other things you can get together – I keep all the things I use when cooking with the children in a special cupboard so they will always know where to find 'their cooking stuff'.

Peppermint Cream Candies

This recipe is ideal to encourage your children to begin having fun in the kitchen. It is the perfect recipe to let them explore their creativity. You may find that they tend to use the dough more like a PlayDoh than something you can eat and will create some really interesting shaped candies.

Ingredients

1 cup confectioners sugar
1 teaspoon peppermint essence
1 egg white
A few drops of food color of your choice (optional)

Method

Sieve the confectioners sugar into a large bowl to remove any lumps.

In another bowl whisk the egg white using a whisk or an electric mixer to create a light, fluffy mix.

Add the peppermint essence and a few drops of food coloring if using and mix well.

Remember that the color will be a lot lighter once added to the confectioners sugar.

Next, slowly pour the mixture into the confectioners sugar and stir well using a spatula (there will be clouds of confectioners sugar if this is not done slowly).

The mixture should be firm enough to come together in a ball.

Tip the dough onto a work surface lightly dusted with icing sugar, roll out to your desired thickness and use interesting cookie cutters to make the candies or encourage the children to make their own shapes. Give them some stuff to decorate the candies if they want to.

Leave for a couple of hours (if the kids will let you) before eating.

Note: You can change this around by adding different flavored essences instead of peppermint.

Strawberry Popsicles

Everyone loves popsicles and most children can't get enough of them. What if your children could make their own at home? This super simple recipe will keep them busy.

Method

1 cup strawberries
4 tablespoon honey
1 teaspoon vanilla essence
A pinch of cinnamon (optional)
4-6 tablespoon water (you could use milk or cream for a creamy popsicle)

Method

Roughly chop the strawberries.

Put the chopped strawberries and water (or milk) into a blender or you could use a stick blender, and blend until the mixture is smooth.

Add the honey, vanilla essence and cinnamon and blend again until thoroughly mixed.

Pour into an ice cube tray and add a small stick, (I use a toothpick) to each section.

Put in the freezer and leave until completely frozen – this will be the hardest bit for your children!

Note: You can use any type of soft fruit for this recipe.

Summer Lemonade

This lemonade recipe is great for children to make for their friends. It is perfect for a summer picnic in the garden or a sleep-over.

Ingredients

2 cups water
1 lemon
Fresh mint leaves
(optional)
Pinch of salt
6 tablespoons sugar
4 ice cubes
Few slices lemon for garnish

Method

Slice the lemon into very thin slices.

Pour the water into a suitable sized jug and add the lemon slices.

Refrigerate and let it soak for 2 hours.

Add the salt, mint, sugar and ice cubes to it and give it a good stir.

Let it rest in the refrigerator for another 30 minutes.

Add the lemon slices, stir well and serve fresh.

Note: Increase the ingredients to make a larger amount for more people. To make a slightly sparkling lemonade use 2 cups of sparking water but just use half a cup to soak the lemon and add the remaining sparkling water just before serving – a bit like making lemon squash.

Ping Pong Candy

This candy looks like small ping pong balls and tastes delicious. The wonderful blend of vanilla with coconut flakes makes it really yummy. Children love making these for birthday parties and sleep-overs.

Ingredients

¼ cup butter, softened
½ (8 ounce) pack of cream cheese
1 teaspoon vanilla extract
4 cups confectioners' sugar
2½ cups flaked coconut
1 tablespoon sprinkles – you choose what kind

Method

Put the butter and cream cheese into a mixing bowl.

Beat together using a hand mixer until the mixture is super smooth.

Stir in the confectioners sugar and add in the vanilla.

Beat again until the sugar is completely incorporated.

Add in the flaked coconut and stir well.

Now create little ping pong balls.

Roll the ping pong balls in the sprinkles.

Leave in refrigerator for 15 minutes. They are now ready to eat.

Note: For an extra bit of fun, instead of the sprinkles you could use popping candy to roll your ping pong candy balls in.

No Bake Granola Bars

This healthy chocolate chip bar is possibly the easiest to make and tastes amazing. The addition of flaxseed, peanut butter and oats makes it crunchy, the cranberries and almonds add the flavor.

Ingredients

2 cups rolled oats
1¼ cups natural crunchy peanut butter
1 cup ground flaxseed
¾ cup honey
¾ cup dried cranberries
½ cup chocolate chips
¼ cup sliced almonds

Method

Put the flax seed and oats in a large mixing bowl and stir.

Next add the cranberries, almonds and chocolate chips and mix well.

Add the peanut butter and honey.

Mix until the ingredients are evenly dispersed then place the mixture in a baking tray lined with plastic wrap to make it easier to remove.

Spend a little time flattening out the top using a spatula. If you want you can sprinkle a few extra chocolate chips over the top and lightly press them down so they will stick to the mixture.

You could also melt some chocolate in the microwave and drizzle randomly over the top of the mixture.

Refrigerate for about 2 hours.

Cut into slices and serve or store in an airtight container.

Note: You can cut these into small squares and call them 'Granola Candies'.

Chocolate Crunchies

Children love to create their own chocolate cakes, and if the recipe is this simple and relatively mess free, any parent would love their children to try. These are really good for a birthday party or a sleep-over.

Ingredients

6 cups crispy rice cereal
1 cup white sugar
1 cup peanut butter
1 cup chocolate chips, melted
1 cup light corn syrup
1 cup butterscotch chips, melted (if you can't get these just double up on the chocolate chips)

Method

In a bowl, combine the white sugar with the butterscotch chips and the chocolate chips.

Add the light corn syrup.

Add the peanut butter and stir well until the mixture is smooth.

Finally add your rice cereal and mix.

Take a muffin tin and put a paper cake case in each. Fill with the mixture.

Refrigerate for at least 2 hours.

Crispy Marshmallow Treats

An adult may be needed to supervise the melting of the marshmallows and butter.

Ingredients

¼ cup butter, melted
4 cups miniature marshmallows, melted
5 cups crisp rice cereal

Method

Place the marshmallows in a bowl and microwave until melted. Open the door every 10-20 seconds to avoid them burning.

Combine the melted marshmallows with the crisp rice cereal.

Add the melted butter and stir well.

Place into a baking tray lined with plastic wrap and refrigerate for at least 2 hours.

Remove from refrigerator, peel off the plastic wrap and cut into little squares.

Note: You could add a selection of chopped nuts and dried fruit to these for an extra bit of texture.

Peanut Butter and Jelly Sandwich Roll

This is a recipe that children can make alone and use their imagination for the filling. Really good for a kids party.

Ingredients

2 slices of bread (brown or white - your preference)
Peanut Butter
Raspberry Jelly

Method

Place the bread slices on a flat surface and roll out until quite thin.

On one side of each slice spread the peanut butter and jelly.

Roll the first slice up tightly with the filling inside then roll the second slice around the first to make one fat roll.

At this point you could make a simple icing with water and confectioners sugar and drizzle randomly over the roll. Allow the icing to set.

Slice into circles and arrange on a plate.

Enjoy!

Note: The filling can be changed for anything that spreads; chocolate spread, Nutella, mashed banana, tuna and mayonnaise, cheese spread, pate etc. – obviously the savory ones wouldn't have the icing. Let your children use their imagination.

Puffed Rice Balls

Puffed rice balls are great to serve at your children's play dates - in fact it's a wonderful recipe for your children and their friends to make *during* their play dates. It will keep them busy and they can eat the results of their labors. Adult supervision will be needed to melt the sugar and butter.

Ingredients

1 cup puffed rice
4 tablespoon honey
1 tablespoon butter
1 tablespoon brown sugar, melted
A pinch of cinnamon

Method

Put the puffed rice into a bowl. Melt the butter in the microwave and add to the puffed rice.

Melt the brown sugar and add to the bowl. Add the honey and cinnamon and mix well.

Form the mixture into small balls and place in paper cake cases.

Refrigerate for 30 - 40 minutes until firm.

Strawberry Ice Cream Popsicles

Everyone loves ice cream and this is so simple that children can easily make it without adult help.

Ingredients

1 cup strawberries
1 cup yoghurt
Few drops of vanilla extract
6 tablespoons honey

Method

Put the strawberries in a bowl and mash them very finely using a fork or get your hands in and squash them (this is the method most kids prefer...).

Add the yoghurt and stir until the mixture is smooth.

Add the vanilla and honey and mix well.

Pour into ice cube tray and put a wooden stick into each cube. You could use eggcups or your own popsicle molds for a larger popsicle.

Put in freezer until frozen.

Note: You can use any soft fruit for this recipe.

Bread Pizza

Who doesn't love pizza? Your children will love to create their own using a variety of toppings. You provide the toppings to choose from so the children can design their very own 'pizza'. The ingredients list below is one that my family like to use, but you can choose your own if you prefer. Adult supervision will be required if the children are making the cooked version.

Ingredients

4 slices of white bread
2 tablespoon tomato sauce
Tomatoes – thinly sliced
Fresh grated cheese
2 cooked sausages
A pinch of paprika
1 tablespoon olive oil (optional)

Method

Remove the crusts from the bread and place on a baking sheet.

Spread each one with tomato sauce making sure to go right up to the edge, then sprinkle with a little grated cheese.

Thinly slice the sausages and arrange on top of the cheese followed by the tomatoes.

Top with the a little more grated cheese and sprinkle with paprika.

Drizzle the olive oil on top (if using) and place in a hot oven until cheese is melted and bubbling.

Alternatively your children could eat their 'pizza' without any cooking at all as long as your toppings are pre-cooked but toast the bread before adding toppings.

You could exchange the white bread for pitta bread or tortilla wraps.

Note: This is a great way to encourage children to try things they wouldn't normally eat. Thinly sliced peppers, cooked vegetables, pineapple, chopped cooked ham, cooked mushrooms, prawns, shrimps, alfalfa sprouts, herbs, scallions etc. are good things to offer for the topping.

Berry Delight

This is a very good and tasty dessert for both grown-ups and children, I love it. Any sort of soft fruit works well.

Ingredients

1 cup raspberries
1 cup blueberries
2 cups Greek yoghurt
Maple syrup
Chocolate shavings

Method

Chop the raspberries and blueberries coarsely.

In a pretty serving glass (the plastic picnic type are ideal for children), place some yoghurt then add a layer of blueberry.

Add another layer of yoghurt then add a layer of raspberries, followed by another layer of yoghurt.

You can have as many layers as you like but remember to finish with a yoghurt layer.

Drizzle some maple syrup on top and sprinkle with the chocolate shavings.

Note: For a more decadent dessert for a grown-up treat, use thick cream instead of Greek yoghurt.

Chicken Vegetable Noodles with Peanut Dressing

This is your children's opportunity to produce a delicious supper for the whole family. It's simple to make but very tasty to eat.

Ingredients

1 pack thin rice noodles
2 cooked boneless chicken breasts
1 carrot
1 cucumber
½ cup sweetcorn kernels (frozen or canned)
½ cup smooth peanut butter
2 tablespoons low-sodium soy sauce
Cold water

Method

Place the noodles in a large bowl and cover with hot water, tap water will do. Leave to soak until soft. Drain and put to one side.

Shred the chicken meat into strips. Using a vegetable peeler, make long, thin strips of the carrot and cucumber.

Put the peanut butter, soy sauce, and 6 tablespoons cold water into a bowl and whisk until smooth. Pour the dressing into a small jug.

Place the noodles, shredded chicken, carrot, sweetcorn and cucumber into a large serving bowl and toss carefully to avoid breaking up the noodles.

Let everyone help themselves to the Chicken Vegetable Noodles, then drizzle with as much peanut dressing as each person prefers.

Chocolate Brownie in a Mug

A delicious but simple chocolate cake and all made in a mug – so not much cleaning up!

Ingredients

¼ cup sugar
¼ cup flour
2 tablespoons cocoa powder
Pinch salt
2 tablespoon olive oil
3 tablespoon water
Teaspoon of confectioners sugar for dusting

Method

Put all the dry ingredients to a large (microwaveable) mug. Add the oil and water and mix until smooth with no lumps.

Place into the microwave for around 1 minute 20 seconds, depending on your microwave.

Remove from microwave, being very careful because the mug will be hot.

Allow to cool slightly then dust with confectioners sugar.

Add a scoop of ice cream or a spoonful of heavy cream and enjoy.

Note: For an extra chocolatey surprise push a square of chocolate into the middle of the mixture before you put it in the microwave.

Chocolate Chip Berry Meringue

This recipe may need adult help if your children are to make their own meringue but you could provide them with the ready-made meringue nests that are easily available so they can make these without any help. Get your children to make these for the next family gathering, your relatives will be suitably impressed!

Ingredients

1/8 cup powdered sugar
1 small egg white
Dash of cream of tartar
Dash of salt
½ tablespoon semisweet chocolate chips
1/8 teaspoon vanilla extract
¼ teaspoon granulated sugar
¼ cup your favorite berries, sliced
Whipped cream

Method

Preheat oven to 250° F. Using a pencil, draw a 3-inch circle on the parchment paper and lay over baking sheet, drawn side down.

Put the egg white, cream of tartar, and salt into a small bowl and beat with an electric mixer at high speed. Then add the powdered sugar, about a tablespoon at a time, beating well after each addition until glossy stiff peaks form. Stir in the vanilla and chocolate chips.

Place a spoonful of the beaten egg white on the drawn circle and spread to shape with a spoon.

Bake in the oven for 60-80 minutes until firm to the touch. Turn off the oven and let the meringue stay in the oven for at least 2-3 hours.

In a bowl, mix together the berries and sugar. Carefully remove the meringue from the paper and place in a serving plate. Spread with whipped cream then top with the berry mixture. Sprinkle with a little confectioners sugar for a finishing touch.

The beauty of this recipe is you can use any berry you like or even combine a few different ones for an added bit of luxury.

Note: These look really good with chocolate shavings sprinkled over the top.

Coconut Chocolate Balls

These little candies are no-bake and require little preparation.

They would be nice for your children to put into small paper cases, then into a cellophane bag tied with a ribbon bow and given as a gift.

If you're not confident letting your children loose with a blender this recipe may need an adult to help prepare the dough – then let the children roll and decorate.

Ingredients

3 tablespoons pitted dates
1 tablespoon coconut butter or regular butter if you can't get coconut butter
3 tablespoons shredded coconut flakes
2 tablespoons chocolate chips

Method

Put all the ingredients in a blender or better yet a food processor and blend until smooth.

Form the mixture into balls and place on a wax sheet.

If you want a more chocolaty taste feel free to drizzle melted chocolate over them.

Put them in the refrigerator to set for 2 hours or so.

Note: you can roll the balls in cocoa powder, sprinkles, popping candy or shredded coconut for a different finish or you could even make a little icing to drizzle over them – use your imagination and experiment.

Critter Cake

This is a great, fun dish for kids to make. They will take great delight in presenting this to family and friends and love the look on their faces as they spot the critters!

Ingredients

1 to 1¼ lb. pack Oreo cookies
1 (8 oz.) pack cream cheese
½ cup butter, softened
1 cup powdered sugar
3 cups milk
1 (12 oz.) tub Cool Whip (you could use chocolate)
2 (3½ oz.) pack instant vanilla or chocolate pudding
½ tsp. vanilla
A few gummy critters
Cocoa powder for dusting

Method

Put the Oreos into a plastic bag and crush with a rolling pin until all cookies are crumbs – your children will love this bit!

Put one third of the crushed Oreos into new, clean flower pots (this is the 'soil'). Put to one side.

Mix butter, cream cheese and sugar and vanilla together. Put to one side.

Combine milk and pudding mix. Fold Cool Whip into the pudding.

Fold together pudding mixture and butter-cream cheese mixture.

Put around one third of this mixture onto the crumbled cookies in the pot. Next, add another layer of cookie crumbs, then pudding mixture etc. continuing until all ingredients are used.

As you're layering the ingredients, place several of the gummy critters in the mixture to replicate a garden of critters. Leave one sticking out of the top for an extra surprise.

Chill in refrigerator for 3 to 4 hours and add a light dusting of cocoa powder before serving.

Crispy Rice and Marshmallow Treats

This family favorite is really easy to make. The ingredient list below is simply a suggestion, you could leave out the almonds and apricots and add your own favorites.

Ingredients

4 cups milk chocolate melts
½ cup butter
3 cups Rice cereal
Small packet mini marshmallows (around 4oz)
½ cup slivered almonds
½ cup finely chopped dried apricots

Method

Line a square cake pan with baking paper or plastic wrap.

Put the chocolate melts and butter in a large bowl and microwave until melted. Stir until smooth.

Stir in remaining ingredients and mix until everything is well combined.

Spread mixture into a baking pan lined with plastic wrap making sure it is as level as you can. At this point you could sprinkle grated chocolate over the top or any other decoration you fancy. You could even drizzle with a simple icing.

Refrigerate until firm then cut into squares. Remove from pan and store in an airtight container in the refrigerator.

Note: Instead of using a cake pan you could put a spoonful of the mixture into paper cake cases to make individual cakes.

Sweet Marshmallow Candy

These candies are easy to make and kids can make them alone – it may be a bit messy so aprons are a must!

Ingredients

15 large marshmallows, quartered
15 cookies
1 cup chopped nuts
2/3 cup sweetened condensed milk
1 cup desiccated coconut

Method

Put the cookies into a ziplock bag and crush with a rolling pin then put them into a large bowl with the coconut.

Add the quartered marshmallows and chopped nuts.

Stir the mixture so the ingredients are well dispersed then pour the condensed milk in the bowl and stir again until the mixture is well combined and soft.

Lift the mixture out onto a clean baking tray lined with baking parchment or plastic wrap and flatten it to about 1 inch thick. At this point you can add some decoration, for example sprinkles, more chopped nuts, chocolate shavings etc.

Place in the fridge for 2 to 3 hours.

Once chilled and set, cut into squares.

Note: You could use mini marshmallows instead of the large ones and cut with shaped cookie cutters when set.

Quick Nut Cookies

Ingredients

1 cup your choice of nuts (you can use just one type or a mixture)
1 cup pitted dates
2 tablespoons cocoa powder
3 tablespoons honey
1 tablespoon butter, melted

Method

Blend the nuts into rough crumbs but not too fine, put into a bowl.

Next blend the dates and put into the bowl with nuts.

Mix the nuts and the dates, sprinkle the cocoa powder over the date and nut mixture and stir, next add the honey and melted butter and mix until all ingredients are well combined.

Taste and add more honey for more sweetness if you like – you decide.

Spread the mixture in a baking pan lined with plastic wrap.

Obviously the smaller the pan, the thicker
the cookie so you choose the size.

Put in the fridge to chill for around 1 hour.

Cut into squares or you could use interesting
shaped cookie cutters for fun cookies.

Cupcake Fun

As the name suggests this recipe means that your kids can have some fun with cupcakes.

I usually make some cupcakes ahead of time so the children can do the decorating but you can buy them if you prefer.

Ingredients

12 plain undecorated cupcakes
Selection of icing
Selection of sprinkles

Method

There isn't really a method here, you can do exactly as you want.

The beauty of this is that you don't need to go through the process of making the cupcakes if you haven't the time and the plain, undecorated ones are usually really inexpensive.

Give the children lots of different things to choose from to decorate the cupcakes.

You can also buy some **cookies** and make a simple butter cream to sandwich two cookies together. Then decorate with icing and sprinkles. You can let the children color the icing themselves with food coloring, you will get some very interesting iced cupcakes...

Get some prepared marzipan and show your children how to make leaves etc. for decoration. They could use food coloring to make the leaves green.

For an instant treat use vanilla ice cream to sandwich the cookies together.

Children absolutely love making these because they need the very minimum help from an adult and they can use their imagination to create their very own special cupcakes or decorated cookies.

Quick and Easy Raspberry Mousse

This berry mousse is so simple to make and a real crowd pleaser. Get the children to make this for all the family.

Ingredients

10oz raspberries
2½oz golden caster sugar
Pot Greek yogurt
2 medium egg whites

Method

Put the raspberries into a food processor with the sugar and blend together until smooth or simply squish with clean hands.

Press through a sieve to remove the pips.

Stir in the Greek yogurt.

Whisk the egg whites to soft peaks and fold into the yogurt/raspberry berry mixture.

Spoon into 4 glasses. Chill for 1-2 hours.
Serve topped with a couple of whole
raspberries.

Use frozen berries (you'll have to blitz with a
blender) and serve immediately as a soft-
whip raspberry ice cream.

Note: You can use any soft fruit for this
recipe.

Oatmeal and Chocolate Orange Cookies

Ingredients

1 tablespoon cocoa
2 cups sugar
1 cup chocolate chips
½ stick butter or margarine
3½ cups oats
1 teaspoon vanilla extract
1 cup shredded coconut
3 tablespoons peanut butter
Zest and juice of 1 orange

Method

Melt the butter, peanut butter, chocolate chips and zest together in a microwave. Add the vanilla extract, sugar and orange juice. Stir until the sugar has dissolved.

Sprinkle the cocoa powder over and stir again. Add the oats and shredded coconut and mix until everything is thoroughly combined.

Drop spoonfuls of the mixture onto a clean baking pan or into paper cake cases and place in the refrigerator until set.

Easy Tortilla Lunch

This is a quick and easy lunch that children can prepare themselves. The ingredient list below is just  a suggestion, you decide what you want to use to fill your tortilla.

Ingredients

2 flour tortillas
Mayonnaise
2 slices of cooked ham
Grated cheese
Tomatoes
Lettuce
Peppers

Method

Lay the tortillas side by side on a worktop.

With the back of a spoon, spread each with mayonnaise right to the edges – as much or as little as you prefer.

Down the center of the tortilla sprinkle with grated cheese. Then add the rest of your chosen ingredients to the center of the tortilla.

Bring the bottom of the tortilla up over the ingredients and bring both sides to the middle overlapping.

Arrange on serving plate and enjoy.

Chocolate Marshmallow Lollipops

This recipe is great fun when you provide a good selection of decoration stuff for your children to choose from. Below is a short list of some of the things I provide for my grandchildren when they want to make these.

Ingredients

Large marshmallows
Small sticks (I use toothpicks)
A bowl of melted chocolate
A selection of sprinkles – hundreds and thousands, chocolate sprinkles, crushed nuts, finely shredded coconut, different colored sprinkles (gold and silver color are the most popular in my house), brown sugar etc.
Different colored icing – you can buy ready-made icing in a tube.

Method

Push a small stick into each marshmallow.

Dip each marshmallow into the melted chocolate then into the sprinkles.

Sit on a sheet of waxed paper until the chocolate has set – about 30 minutes.

If you are using icing, now is the time to do it. Either drizzle randomly with a simple icing or give your children a tube of the ready-made icing and they can write their initials on the marshmallows, or they can personalize each one to give as a gift.

If you want to add these to a pack of candies that your children are making for a gift, remove the stick and put each finished marshmallow into a small paper cake case.

Ricotta Strawberry Trifle

This is a dessert that children can make on their own. The recipe is for a single serving so simply double up if you want more servings.

Ingredients

1/3 cup strawberries
½ tablespoon finely chopped mint (optional)
1/3 cup fat free Ricotta cheese
1 tablespoon whipping cream
1 trifle finger or any other biscuit cookie
1 teaspoon sugar
1/3 teaspoon vanilla extract
1 tablespoon chopped nuts (optional)

Method

Slice the strawberries and put in a bowl, stir in the chopped mint and set aside.

In a separate bowl, mix together the cheese, whipping cream, sugar and vanilla until smooth.

Crush the cookie or trifle finger.

Place a layer of the prepared ricotta mixture in the bottom of a glass mold.

Sprinkle the cookie crumbles over it. Top with another layer of ricotta mixture followed by the strawberry and mint mixture.

Finally, top with the remaining ricotta mix and sprinkle with chopped nuts.

Serve immediately or let chill for 30 - 60 minutes and then enjoy.

Note: The beauty of this recipe is you can add anything you like – design your own dessert! The trifle in the photo was topped with blueberries because I love them and I omitted the mint. I also substituted the crushed cookie for thinly sliced butter brioche.

Chocolate Peanut Butter Balls

Ingredients

4 teaspoons peanut butter
1 tablespoon softened butter
¼ cup (slightly heaping) powdered sugar
¼ cup semisweet chocolate chips
Any decoration you fancy – sprinkles, coconut, cocoa powder – use your imagination.

Method

In a small bowl combine the butter and peanut butter.

Mix well until smooth and creamy. Add the powdered sugar and mix well.

Shape into small balls.

In a microwave safe bowl melt the chocolate chips.

Gently coat the balls with chocolate and dip in your chosen decoration (if you want to decorate).

Let stand for a while until the chocolate is
set.

Note: Another one for the candy gift bag!

White Chocolate Cake Balls

These are really simple to make and children love to get involved.

Ingredients

1 plain cake
1 container frosting – any flavor you like
White chocolate chips
Sprinkles for decoration

Method

In a bowl, break up the cake into crumbs.

Add the container of frosting and mix well. Leave in the refrigerator for at least a couple of hours.

Using an ice cream scoop or, if you want smaller candies, a melon baller, scoop out small balls of the mixture and place on a sheet of waxed paper.

Melt the chocolate in a bowl in the microwave.

Dip each of the cake balls into the chocolate and leave on wax paper for a few minutes then dip into the sprinkles.

Leave for a couple of hours until completely set.

Note: An interesting and fun variation for this recipe is to pack the frosting and cake mixture into sugar cones, drizzle some melted chocolate on top and add sprinkles before putting in the refrigerator to set.

Banana Peanut Tortilla

These are a great addition to a picnic or a school lunch box and quick and easy to make.

Ingredients

Flour tortilla
Peanut butter
Banana

Method

This doesn't need much description – it's so easy!

Place the tortilla on a flat surface and spread liberally with peanut butter right to the edge.

Place the banana at one end and roll tightly – done!

Note: You could add some raspberry jelly to spread with the peanut butter or use honey instead of the peanut butter.

Ask the children to think of different things to spread on the tortilla, you may be surprised when they come up with ideas you had never even thought of.

Fruit and Jello Cones

These jello cones are easy to make and fun to eat. They will keep in the refrigerator for a few days too.

Ingredients

Sugar cones
Sheet of gelatin
Few drops food coloring
Soft fruit – strawberries, raspberries, blueberries etc.
Squirty cream
Sprinkle to decorate

Method

Place each sugar cone in a tall glass or something to keep them upright and stable.

Melt the gelatin according to packet instruction and leave to cool. Add a few drops of food coloring stir well to disperse evenly.

Meanwhile chop your fruit into bite sized pieces and drop some into each cone. Top up with the cool, colored gelatin. If the gelatin is not cool enough the cones will go soggy.

Leave to set. When ready to eat top with a squirt of cream and sprinkles.

Note: You could replace the squirty cream with ice cream.

Quick Chocolate Orange Fudge

This has got to be the quickest, cheapest and easiest fudge to make a home. You only need three ingredients and about 5 minutes to make this.

Ingredients

3 x 6oz packets of chocolate chips
Can of condensed milk
Orange flavoring

Method

Pour all the chocolate chips into a large bowl and melt in the microwave.

Stir until smooth then add a few drops of orange flavoring, stir again and taste to make sure you have enough orange flavor. Remember to add only a few drops at a time – you can keep adding but you can't take it out if you put in too much...

Pour the whole of the can of condensed milk into the chocolate and stir well.

Line a cake pan with either plastic wrap or parchment paper and pour the mixture in.

Work the mixture into the corners and smooth until the top is as flat as you can get it.

Refrigerate for around 4 hours or until set. Remove from pan, peel off the paper and cut into small squares or you could even use a small cookie cutter to make interesting fudge shapes.

Note: Now you have the basic recipe you can use your imagination and change things around a bit.

You could use vanilla flavoring or whatever takes your fancy. You could also use white chocolate chips for a bit of variety.

Party Sandwich Fun

Another super simple recipe where your children get to use their imagination – with your help of course.

It is great fun to help prepare these unique sandwiches for a birthday party, a picnic or a family get together.

Ingredients

4 slices of wholewheat bread
A selection of fillings
A selection of cookie cutters in different shapes

Method

From the ingredient list you can tell that this is very much a 'make up your own' type of recipe.

Butter one side of the bread if you wish. Make your sandwich with whatever filling you choose – I usually put three or four different fillings in dishes for the children to choose from and some salad ingredients to use if they want. Good fillings are tuna and mayonnaise, peanut butter and jelly, prawns and mayonnaise, ham and sweet pickle, cooked chicken. Your family may like something different; ask the children what they would like in their sandwiches.

Press the sandwich down firmly then, using a cookie cutter, cut the sandwiches into shapes.

Arrange on a serving plate and cover with plastic wrap until ready to eat.

Healthy Cheese and Tuna Tortilla Lunch

This quick and easy lunch is fabulous for letting your children try ingredients that they wouldn't normally even look at. The ingredient list is simply a suggestion, you choose what to you prepare for the children to fill their tortilla with.

Ingredients

Flour tortillas
Selection of salad leaves
Tomatoes
Asparagus tips, cooked
Thinly sliced yellow or green peppers
Cream cheese – you could try Brie or Camembert
1 can tuna in brine or spring water
Squares of foil

Method

Place the flour tortillas on a flat surface and, with the back of a spoon or a palette knife, spread your chosen cream cheese over the entire tortilla.

Next drain the tuna well. Begin to add your chosen ingredients down the center of each tortilla leaving the tuna until last.

When you are satisfied with the ingredients, bring the bottom of the tortilla up then fold the sides to the center with a small overlap.

To prevent a well-filled tortilla from springing open, stick a cocktail stick or kebab stick through while you prepare all the tortillas you need.

To make the tortillas easier to eat, wrap the bottom end of the tortilla in foil, arrange on plate and enjoy.

This is a lovely fresh, healthy lunch the children can prepare with minimum of help.

Chocolate Peanut Butter Squares

Quick and easy to make,

Ingredients

1 cup butter or margarine, melted
2 cups graham cracker crumbs
2 cups confectioners' sugar
1½ cup peanut butter
1½ cups semisweet chocolate chips
4 tablespoons peanut butter

Method

In a medium bowl, mix together the butter or margarine, graham cracker crumbs, confectioners' sugar, and ½ cup of the peanut butter until well blended. Press evenly into the bottom of an ungreased cake pan.

Melt the chocolate chips in the microwave with the remaining peanut butter, stirring occasionally until smooth. Spread over the prepared crust.

Refrigerate for at least one hour before cutting into squares.

Note: You could sprinkle with chopped nuts, mini marshmallows or un-melted chocolate chips before putting in the refrigerator.

Easy Nutella Cheesecake

This is a very easy to make cheesecake that children can make for a family get together or a holiday celebration. The children make these in individual dishes so each one can add the decoration they want – saves heated discussions... ☺

Ingredients

For the Base

12 Oreo Cookies or Graham crackers
3 tablespoons butter

For the Filling

1 (8 ounce) package cream cheese, softened
2/3 cup Nutella
1 teaspoon vanilla extract
1 (8 ounce) tub frozen whipped topping, thawed

Method

Put the cookies in a plastic bag and bash with a rolling pin or the bottom of a saucepan until you have a bag of fine crumbs. Melt the butter in the microwave then add the cookie crumbs. Stir until the butter is mixed well into the cookie crumbs.

Divide the base mixture between 4 dishes and press firmly into the bottom of the dish (dishes are better than glasses because there is more surface to spread the base mixture and it is easier to eat from a dish), leave to one side.

Using an electric mixer, beat together the cream cheese and Nutella until very smooth. Add vanilla and mix to combine. Fold in the whipped topping until it is all well mixed in.

Spoon the mixture into the serving bowls on top of the crust. Cover with plastic wrap and refrigerate for at least 3 hours before serving.

Just before serving you can add any decoration you fancy – popping candy is a favorite in my house, but you could simply dust with confectioners sugar, add sprinkles, shaved chocolate curls etc. Let the children use their imagination.

Breakfast Muesli

This is a great way to get your children to eat a healthy breakfast because they will have chosen only their own favorite ingredients to add. The ingredients list below is simply a suggestion of the things you can offer for the children to add to their own personal Breakfast Muesli.

Ingredients

Oat Flakes
Dried apricots
Dried banana
Dried Apple
Raisins
Sultanas
Hazelnuts – chopped
Sliced almonds
Chocolate chips
Chopped dates
Sunflower seeds
Pine nuts
Etc, etc.

Method

Take one cereal container with a lid per child and get them to add a base of oat flakes or you could use rye flakes or wheat flakes – all muesli have some sort of base ingredient. The proportion of the base ingredient is not really important just make sure there is sufficient in the container.

Now it's time for the fun. The children can begin to add their own favorite ingredients to make their own personal breakfast.

Add the chosen ingredients a tablespoonful at a time. Once the children have added everything they like put the lids on the container and shake all the ingredients together. This will store for around a month if kept in the airtight container – depending of course, on the ingredients you have used.

Note: If there is more than one child involved in making their own breakfast muesli don't forget to label the containers with the child's name or a war could break out...

Some Simple Conversion Figures

IMPERIAL TO METRIC

1 oz = 30g
4 oz = 110g
1lb   = 450g

1 fl.oz = 30ml
5 fl.oz or ¼ pt = 150ml
20 fl.oz or 1pt = 600ml

OVEN TEMPERATURES

130C = 110C fan = 250F = Gas mark 1
150C = 130C fan = 300F = Gas mark 2
170C = 150C fan = 325F = Gas mark 3
180C = 160C fan = 350F = Gas mark 4
190C = 170C fan = 375F = Gas mark 5
200C = 180C fan = 400F = Gas mark 6
220C = 200C fan = 425F = Gas mark 7
230C = 210C fan = 450F = Gas mark 8
240C = 220C fan = 475F = Gas mark 9

AMERICAN SPOON MEASURES

1 level tablespoon flour = 15g flour
1 heaped tablespoon flour = 28g flour

1 level tablespoon sugar = 28g sugar
1 level tablespoon butter = 15g butter

AMERICAN LIQUID MEASURES

1 cup US = 240ml
1 pint US = 480ml
1 quart US = 950ml

AMERICAN SOLID MEASURES

1 cup flour = 125g flour
1 cup butter = 225g butter
1 cup brown sugar = 170g brown sugar
1 cup granulated sugar = 170g granulated
sugar
1 cup icing sugar = 100g icing sugar
1 cup uncooked rice = 170g rice
1 cup chopped nuts = 100g chopped nuts
1 cup fresh breadcrumbs = 150g fresh
breadcrumbs
1 cup sultanas = 140g sultanas

Thank you

Thank you for buying this book and I really hope you and your children will have a lot of fun trying these recipes.

A lot of these recipes are easy to adapt to create something completely unique, so use your imagination and change things around a bit to create your favorite recipes – that's how Family Favorites are born.

I have tried to include some fun recipes that most children will be able to enjoy making but if I have missed your favorite and you would like it included in my next 'No Cook Children's Recipes' book please do send me an email.

penny@cookingwithpenelope.com

If you would like notification of my next cookbook please send an email to the above address and just say you would like notification and I'll make sure you get advanced notice of publication.

I really hope you enjoyed this book and you will use it to have fun with your children. I would really appreciate it if you could leave a review on Amazon.com to let others know what you think about it.

Again, thank you so much and enjoy cooking with your children.

Penny

"No-one is born a great cook, one learns by doing"

~ Julia Child

Notes